An Old Man Sails a Paper Boat

An Old Man Sails a Paper Boat

A Chapbook

PETER WELTNER

marrowstone press

Table of Contents

I.

The Juniper Tree 1
Memnon 2
November Woods in Upstate New York 3
The Wanderer, for David Morris 4
Green Brook Park 5
Stridulation 6
A Cold Light in Connecticut 7
My Father's Last Words 8
Portrait of an Old Man 9
Passages 10
After an Anonymous Poem in an Anthology of Classic Chinese Poetry 12
After an Anonymous Poem in the Greek Anthology 13

II.

Baldur 17
Hebrides 18
In Sorrento 19
A Splinter from the True Cross 20
Richard's Dormition 21
Jim and Glen, Glen and Jim 22
To Karl 24
Politics 25
An Old Man Sails a Paper Boat 26
Homecoming 27
A Letter from Savannah 28
A Summer Day in Carolina 29

I

The Juniper Tree

An owl flying higher with a writhing vole
in its beak might signify nothing more
than an owl's need to eat, like a toll
both pay just for living. A boy watches it soar

into its nest in a hoary old juniper tree
to enjoy it, the furry vole devoured
fast and whole. The tree's roots look scarily
like ogres' feet, its limbs projected

out like knotty fingers that would catch him
if they could. Maybe it is only a whim
of deep woods and a quickening night
that the thrice-hidden moon glares white

as sun upon snow or river's ice. Beneath
his feet, the boy spies slivers of bone
clean and sharp as a small child's teeth
or quartz chips polished on a whetstone,

the child, the child who's buried in no graveyard
weeping while a thick mist blows through
the wilderness, his way home barred
by darkness as a keen owl hoots who-who, who-who.

Memnon

At first light, I've read, the Colossi of Memnon
sing a plaint, harmonious yet, in some sense,
also tragic. Pilgrims to this day, as the sun
rises there, gather in the desert heat, too intense
to stay long, to hear dawn strike the massive
stone statues of Amenhotep into the song
one devotee has said sounds like a lamentation,
a grieving mother's keening that she must outlive
her son or daughter. I do not know if it is wrong
to worship the restoration of light. Today, the sun
rose late through fog over our plague ridden city,
red as the fires consuming the wilderness not far
north of us. Nor do I know much about tragedy.
My life has been mostly happy. But it looked like a scar
in the sky, that sun, and the song it sang lacked mercy.

.

November Woods in Upstate New York

Granitic black beetles lumber under rocks. Ants
in tribes, white grubs, milky caterpillars,
slick footlong bloodworms. Twining plants,
wild ivy, honeysuckle, wood fern, shrub junipers
threading in and out of brush land. A spider
knits its web among dew wet twigs that glint
in the moonlight. A snake, still awake, slithers
toward water. A creek ripples. There's a hint
of winter in the air, like the glow of a forest after
first snow. Remember, a whippoorwill flying over
my head sings to me still, remember me, child,
when you've grown old and suspicious of the wild
places in your heart you thought you'd lost. Remember
Eden. Insects' buzzing. Starlight seeping through poplar
leaves. The rustle of night creatures. Creation astir forever.

The Wanderer, for David Morris

After his long walk back from a tough trek on a wet,
muggy, summer evening, the doubts return,
as they always do after a day spent in the sweat
and strain of wilderness, what he comes to learn
from woods by looking, reality too visible maybe,
everything simply what it is, each fern, each tree,
rock, boulder, cooling pool, waterfall, fast coursing
creek, the sun blank white at noon, its fierce light
piercingly hot, the rank rot of a fox hide—nothing
is not sure, the path underfoot, the birds, the canopy,
route and way, no need for words as he moves easily
through its world undeterred by the goalessness
of wandering far off trail, the loveliness that can be
found through the solitude of a forest, the profundity
it silences if twice asked why, like an Absolute's muted Yes.

.

Green Brook Park

A boy playing on a playground swing,
his older sister on a teeter-totter,
their mother, father giddily spinning
round and round until they blur

together like figures on a top
whirling into obscurity
as it spirals, with nowhere to stop,
out of control, this memory

of me, my family on a Saturday
in the park I see, bleary-
eyed, as if we were four
swallows flying into a cloudy sky

or the shallow creek in the park I'd play
in late, needing to stay,
to see where it went,
trickling on my feet, intent

on steadily flowing. What had it meant,
that morning, my mother's offering
her hand to a fluttering,
hovering eastern tiger swallow tail,

the lone image, the one detail
of my boyhood I remember
as serene: the yellow-green jade ring
on her finger the butterfly sipped from like water.

Stridulation

It is late summer fast changing into fall,
half-lit shadows at dusk, birds aloft
in the dying light before the pall
of darkness descends, the sunset soft
as the flames of candles flickering
through trees, tinting their leaves
oak orange, maple red while a breeze
blows through windows with the sting
of October. Cicadas, katydids, crickets
lustily sing their last, raspy choral
music, its buzzing rattle like some skeletal
part scraping bare bone so sharply it sets
the nerves on edge as their dying cries echo
off the hushed walls of woods. What do they know,
before he does, of tomorrow? Of night songs and their call?

A Cold Light in Connecticut

A bird lands on my window
sill, beating its wings,
frantic to get in.
It is winter,

the first day of real snow.
The cold stings
my face. The bird is thin.
It should have flown

south but somehow forgot to.
I cannot change
my dream
to save you,

you the bird I saw
this morning, the strange,
too fast fluttering of your heart,
your clutching claws.

It is always like that
when you fly back
to me. I reach
out to grasp you

while snowflakes, thick and fat,
fall amid cracks
of thunder breaching
the heavens.

It is a familiar tragedy
most suns
wake us to:
you, a famished, wet bird

freezing, pecking at an icy
window pane
I let in
too late.

My Father's Last Words

"…and then I dreamed of clouds opening up and dropping such riches on
me that when I woke up, I cried because I wanted to dream again."

Drayhorses' hooves clop on cobblestones.
Fresh snow in the park, ice floes floating
in the Hudson River. A tugboat groans,
a ship's horns blare, brightly trumpeting

its imminent departure. Sailing to where?
Passengers wave goodbye to families
and friends. A few wait dockside and stare
as the liner heads toward faraway seas,

foreign ports the young boy who watches
has never heard of, though they're calling
to him like the water's plaintive, mournful
splashing on piers as the giant ship vanishes

from sight of the harbor. Where would he go
if he could stow away or fly like a gull,
far as swallows, I ask him. He is slow
to answer, lying in bed in the near charnel

house I've been forced by law to confine him in.
A pink streak of spit oozes down his chin.
I miss Oma, he says, her farm on Staten
Island, her white hair pulled back in a bun,

no pin out of place as she sewed. And the piles
of wood in the bin behind the barn my cousin
and I used to hide in. He looks up at me and smiles.
I'm tired now, son. Let me sleep. Let me go home again.

Portrait of an Old Man

I recall a Rembrandt portrait of an elderly
man he painted when he also was old
that I first saw at the Met years ago
from whose eyes shone a light Caravaggio
saved for young boys' bodies. A tree
when its leaves are failing in autumn, its bold
yellow gleaming colors stolen from the sun
at noon, might reveal in its way the same
intensity as if inside it there were a flame
burning all the brighter before its day is done.
I wonder why it is that youth lingers in
the liminal half-light and shadows of an agèd
man's vision, seeing his life trying to begin
again in the smoldering light by which it is ended.

Passages

1.

A high tide sweeps the beach,
its narrow strand white under
a whiter sky. The waves reach
high as the sea wall, the water

more turbulent by cliffs. Sea
oats tremble, manzanita whips
in the wind, crows grow wary
of grubbing as a storm grips

the coastline. A lone gull slips
through mist while seals sleep
soundly on boulders, logy
and plump. There is nothing deep

to see in this scene: rocks, a gull,
a rising tide, a wind blown tree,
bent low, two late stars dimly
shining, like old men's eyes, fading and wistful.

2.

Needles, leaves. Tree after tree
stitched together. Cone seeds
scattered on duff. Canopy
like a green sky, moss and weeds.

A forest in shadows, sunlight
like gaps, flaws in a tapestry
of oak groves. Autumnal flight
of geese. Wet leaves. A nearby

lake. Intimations, maybe ours,
of hiking through brush
and thickets, the stars
flickering through foliage, the rush

10

of a stream as we pursued its way
in, too deep into wilderness
not to stay there, the lay
of the land ahead not ours to guess.

3.

Above the craggy, rocky shoreline,
where quests are ended,
moss and fern and vine
green with summer as you'd said

you'd remembered, the sun
reflected on the stream
we'd drunk from, where we'd begun
long ago, like a dream

of a trek to somewhere important,
the woods' pale light
like a creek rippling, fluent
and clear as we hiked to the site

where we'd met, far in the forest
you cherished most,
seeking the long rest
we needed when we'd found ourselves lost.

After an Anonymous Poem in an Anthology of Classic Chinese Poetry

To write, compose on water, in the wind-tossed air,
to see in each unfolding spring leaf
the grief
you feel for the friends you've lost, to care
for them past enduring, to despair
of anything's lasting: how bear
it, then, the cry you hear of life ever-thriving deep
in the night and believe a dream, though you never sleep?

Look. Twilight is bestowing its half-lit magnanimity
on you, the grace to come as days march by
in due procession,
chanting, proclaiming in the language
of wine and sunshine, sea-swells, rocks and stones,
of green things soon to die, its hymns to sorrow, its threnodies of change.
.

After an Anonymous Poem in the Greek Anthology

1.

Its throat a golden, feathery orange, its breast downy
red, a bird sings as if to warn the boy of soaring
too high on a backyard swing, to prophesy,
maybe, of dangers lurking ahead, then takes wing,
a beautiful bird gliding on wind while the sun's still
hesitant on the horizon. The dogwood is ready
to burst into bloom, lady's slippers, white jonquil,
jacks-in-the-pulpit. A squirrel, wood mice scurry
through a thicket of fireweed. The earth is worthy
of devotion. Bronze-tipped wild roses. Willows' limbs lazily
drooping as ever, shivering in the chilly breezes, the sky
a deep and serious blue. The chains creaks as the boy
leaps off the swing, briefly suspended in air, as if to free
himself from fear of the life before and after time's while bees,
busily dawn-gathering, buzz past, bearing news of the world and its joys.

2.

His windows flung open, the sun surprises, his view
of the world still raw
perhaps, like a seedling tree in woods

new planted, too fresh, make-do
about its love for light, or the caw-caw
of a solitary crow at dawn waking the neighborhood

early. His young life is passing by him too fast,
like mine or yours
now we've grown old, with the quickness of a flower

the most ancient poetry told us, lamenting how it cannot last,
though dawn still pours
its glories on us, now and in the hour.

II

Baldur

How bitterly cold and white the sun can be
in early evening, though it soon will be set
on fire, raging in splendor until dowsed by the sea.
I think of stories, legends of how, like a debt
they must pay to fate, the Vikings would load
the body of their dead chief and his hoard
onto a longship and burn it as it left land
with his slaves and faithful wife aboard. Just
myths perhaps. No one is here with me, sun
moon low hills cliffs clouds beach where I stand
all blanched by heavy mist and fog, raw as gusts
of wind off Arctic floes blowing through an inlet.
Birds huddle close by ocean's edge, unwilling to fly
when the air feels frozen, hard, white, and cold as the sky
until at sunset it blazes like a longship at its lord's cremation.

Hebrides

Rocks randomly heaped on a dark jagged promontory
jutting far into the sea, shrouded, gauzy
with mist, the sky dun gray. There are few
signs of life and a bracing chill to the morning
that make me shudder, something in the view
along the streams like a will o wisp glowing
on an icy lake. The world appears to be denuded,
stripped to its essence, water, sky, and rocks
so black it might be near midnight, the sun denied
its dawn by a feud between gods. On the other side
of low, rounded, treeless hills, safe from winds, flocks
of sheep graze. I can hear bells tinkle as they're led
out, soft bleating, a dog's barking. Far away, more islands
rise out of the sea, like mounds of massive, sandless strands
of matter. I tell you this to speak of man's loneliness. His stony pride.

.

In Sorrento

Yes, this one, this fist-sized, speckled white stone
he had saved—not pocked, not chipped,
though water- and weather-worn—-
is the heart I'd ripped
out of him, the love he claimed I'd turned cold
and hard as rock. He should have cast it back
into the sea as mere fools' gold,
the seams of light glittering along a crack

I'd exposed only to cheat us both. I should tell
you about how he lived with me
near a cliff where we watched the swells
of lapping waves daily
scatter bones
of birds and fish and the shells

of clams, abalone, and cockles along the Amalfi
coast. Once, in Sorrento
he'd pocketed a handful of stones low
tide had beached after the sea
had washed them to a gemlike purity, to choose
the most perfect of them, the best
of many, he'd said, giving me it after tossing back the rest,
like a relic I needed to seek remission for all I'd made us lose.

A Splinter from the True Cross

The young boy's hair, his slender arms are lightly
powdered with sawdust, his piercing eyes
bird-black and slightly frightened. Passing by, fiery
clouds momentarily glare into his father's workroom,

dank as caves in hills we've played in, shaded by vines
and thickets of brush from sunlight, like a tomb
almost: that dark when we hid there from storms. Shells
and stones from a creek, pine cones, seeds, shrines

to the nature he loved to roam in, lie on a table. As he tries
to remove a splinter from his finger, more blood swells
from the spot, dripping, spilling onto the floor. He looks
up at his mother, a bit scared, glances over as if asking me

to help her as she slowly slips the sliver out. In prophetic books,
one can read how any offhand moment might be premonitory
of great events, of meanings that unfold only after, visionary
in their implications. When I think of Ron's slight wound now,

I wonder if what I saw on her face were the first stirrings of her sorrow
when she heard, a decade later, the fate of her son,
what his mother will come to call the crown of thorns he'd worn
shedding his blood in Khe Sanh for a world ever in need of redemption.

Richard's Dormition

Rick's bedroom grows darker the more ill
he becomes. His body shrivels. Nightmares
haunt him asleep or awake with shrill
voices demanding he save himself. Who dares

defy them, the violent angels of a terror new
to his dying? What comes after, like a vision,
a visitation, a work of grace to subdue
his fears? A Schubert piano sonata, the one

in A major. He asks me to play it for him on
his CD player, in Arrau's performance.
Afterwards, he says he feels freer, reborn
almost as if he might last as perpetually as a dance

survives in Yeats' imagination. Only sex and death
possess the serious mind, Rick quotes, his breath
weaker. He sleeps and leaves the world, his favorite
music, poetry inside him and he far more real and as passionate.

Jim and Glen, Glen and Jim

1.

Dying old man, the one who bears your burdens bears
the weight of everything. As you lie in
your room, the night reflects his fears,
too, the mirror he stares into shedding tears like yours.

2.

The pine grove, the forest you played in as a child,
the meadow with its meandering stream,
the loves fated you the day you were born, wild
in your wanderings, longing to return home even now.

3.

He lifts you up in his arms. Holds you gently like
a mother, the slumped body he embraces,
heavy with the wrongs it carries. He tries to strike
back at the past your tired muscles dare struggle against.

4.

You say to him, "I thought I was all right until
the morning I stumbled down the stairs.
I lied to you when I said I'd tripped. I'm ill
and will keep on falling like that, like Adam, forever."

5.

So weak today, you collapse. A miracle on its own,
lonely, is a miracle that will not work. Trickster,
healer, never weak in spirit, let your husband be known
for the prayers he brings you like rain in springtime gushing.

6.

An agèd man's nakedness is like the sun's. It blinds
the one who gazes on it too long. Like goodness.
Or the waning moon, undone by time. It binds
the body to its old desires, like you ashamed of your dying.

7.

The wordlessness of pain, its solitude, its infamous silence,
the blank nothing of it, its mystery, ineffability,
emptiness, the world's erasure, its transcendence
of everything but itself, your lover appalled by his failures.

8.

He tries to imagine it, to conceive of his own oblivion,
too. Yet it is him imagining it, him in the blank
nothing, as if you were his father, saying, "Is it too late, my son,
for me to make up for all the love I unwittingly forgot to give you?"

9.

Down. Down. Your lover falls as far down as you do. All
the way down. He's leaving town. Moving somewhere
else. He carries what he can of you in his arms. Call
it enough. A watch, a lock of your hair, a sack full of photographs.

10.

And settles, alone, in New Hampshire, in a northern gloom
where the night sky shines on icy fields
brighter than by day. In his new bedroom,
your absence glows as snow, as lost love does, whiter by moonlight.

To Karl

I am watching our movie again in my head
though I can't change how it ends even
in imagination. Love denied. And the lead
left desolate, not knowing how to begin

his life over. Once, on a ship sailing
home, I watched its snowy trail drift
northward until its wake started sinking
into waves ice-capped like the sea I'd seen

in the film, the pallid sky vacant as the screen
it was shown on before the theater
darkened. Sometimes there's a whiteness
to heartache I wish might last forever,

like an empty wall or blank page I project on
whatever I choose to see in redress
for all that's missing, like a misted window grown
so cold I can write your name on it with my breath and a finger.

Politics

The sky is the color of undyed linen with undertones
of gray. The sea by the cliffs is a slick green shiny
as olive leaves on a hot summer day. No one owns
anything here, or so it's proclaimed by the graffiti
white washed on boulders and rock face, protests
scrawled on posts attacking the tyrants in power
in Athens. A gull on a dockside wall watches crests
slap against the rocking hulls of fishing boats, the water
limpid, translucent blue. Why wander the beach
for a few more summers with my stick and dimming
sight? Why wither like a vine on a stake? I reach
out to you, my lost friend Cleisthenes and your two
companions in that land below which allows no singing
or dancing or feasting and yet knows no betrayal: you
who speak of freedom through the silence of your speech.

An Old Man Sails a Paper Boat

Pink-gray clouds drift through the twilit heavens
brightening day's end as they cast shadows on glens
and meadows. Migrating swifts glide, circling
over trees guarding fields like wilderness gardens
of yellow and white daisies, salvia, scarlet poppies,
lupine, rain lilies. Pearly-scaled minnows–darting
this way, that–flash among reeds while a breeze
shakes their grassy thin stems, shimmering like wires
as salmon splash, thrashing up falls. Like leaves,
all life is transient, evanescent. But what he desires
is more than his youth, this old man bewitched by evening.
As it flows past his feet, the creek chatters and chirrups spritely,
happily in last light. He holds a folded paper boat like those he
made as a boy to play with, then lets it go to sail downstream, a stir
in the wind as it drifts toward the river, the sea, like a dream set free on water.

Homecoming

His high school, the classrooms he lingers
in, the wide doors he gazes out, the rusty
sinks in the lab, the gray metal lockers
look the same. The parking lot is as tightly
packed with cars, the yellow school buses
lined up below the football field as antiquated,
the bleachers hard as cement. This is his
world as it was, though the murals have faded
even more since the era of WPA, long before
his time anyway. The chill air is spare, tawny,
the windows burnished by a late October sun
that flames into red over trees. Tonight, a party.
If the power of young lives recalled is a kind of heaven,
he would go and remember, then leave and ask for no more.

A Letter from Savannah

The room was a shambles, shades faded and frayed,
highball glasses shattered against closets, ashtrays
scattered on the floor, a sagging bed left unmade,
shreds of it strewn in pieces on a rug, glaring rays
from passing headlights sneaking through shutters'
broken slats. Everything abused, nothing saved to last
in the sleazy motel our fears had led us to. A shower
stall black with mildew. A sallow plaster wall smashed
in with a fist or shoe's heel. The party-hat lamps. Who
had rented this room before us? No matter. The fever
soaring in us let us ignore the shabby circumstance
where we first saw each other naked on a mattress. Romance
is like that. Blind to torn sheets, blankets, used rubbers
in waste cans, the whole world. Today, I read a letter from you,
forty years later, wondering if I think of us sometimes and remember.

A Summer Day in Carolina

Through clouds, the sun stares into a pool where its reflection
glares back at it stunning as lost wisdom. Noon heat weighs
on the earth heavy as weeks of steady rain. A pair
of buckeye butterflies ripple in a breeze that plays
with them like a cat battering loose a spool of ribbon.
Mist shimmers off the meadows, white and blinding
as day's first light when sleepy eyes waken to morning.
A green lynx spider creeps up an oozing, listing stalk
of milkweed. Blue jays berate a fox squirrel. In the creek,
twigs, winged seeds, the slivery threads of dandelion, chalk
gray reeds drift and twist past sandbars downstream. A red-
shouldered hawk, high up, at the edge of light, glides over
the dark-wooded forest, hunting prey. When I say what I seek
from art is more than I can know or see or words allow to be said,
I mean this, this summer day in Carolina as the sun broke free on its feathers.

Peter Weltner was raised in northern New Jersey and piedmont North Carolina. He graduated from Hamilton College (A.B.) and Indiana University (Ph.D.). For thirty seven years, he taught American, British, and Irish literature at San Francisco State University.

He has published twenty five books or chapbooks of fiction and poetry, and his work over the years has appeared in numerous literary magazines and journals. He was awarded two O. Henrys for his short stories. His most recent titles are *In the Half Light* (Brick House Books), *Bird and Tree/In Place, Scrapbook Mappings of My Country,* and *Woods and the City,* (Marrowstone Press.) He lives with his husband of thirty five years, Atticus Carr, in San Francisco, steps away from the Pacific.

www.ingramcontent.com/pod-product-compliance
Lightning Source LLC
Chambersburg PA
CBHW032134050726
47590CB00008B/3086